The 50 Best Games for **Brain Exercise**

The 50 Best Group Games Pocket Books

The 50 Best Games for Building Self-Esteem
The 50 Best Perception Games
The 50 Best Games for Brain Exercise
The 50 Best Games for Relaxation & Concentration
The 50 Best Games for Speech & Language Development
The 50 Best Games for Children's Groups
The 50 Best Games for Groups
The 50 Best Games for Rainy Days

The 50 Best Games for Brain Exercise

Rosemarie Portmann
translated by Lilo Seelos

HINTONHOUSE

First published in 2008 by

Hinton House Publishers Ltd
Newman House, 4 High Street, Buckingham, MK18 1NT, UK

info@hintonpublishers.com
www.hintonpublishers.com

All rights reserved. The whole of this work, including all text and illustrations, is protected by copyright. No parts of this work may be loaded, stored, manipulated, reproduced, or transmitted in any form or by any means, electronic or mechanical, including photocopying and recording, or by any information, storage and retrieval system without prior written permission from the publisher, on behalf of the copyright owner.

© 2008 Hinton House Publishers Ltd

Printed in the United Kingdom by Hobbs the Printers Ltd

British Library Cataloguing in Publication Data
Portmann, Rosemarie
  The 50 best games for brain exercise. – (The 50 best group games pocket books ; v. 3)
  1. Brain 2. Intellect 3. Group games
  I. Title II. Brain exercise III. The fifty best games for brain exercise
  153.9

ISBN-13: 9781906531140

Originally published in German by Don Bosco Verlag München under the title *Die 50 besten Spiele zum Gehirnjogging*
© Don Bosco Verlag, München 2005

Contents

Games for Attention & Concentration
  1 Everyday Observations
  2 Feeling is Everything
  3 Perceiving With All the Senses
  4 Souvenirs
  5 Mum Likes Coffee
  6 Obviously
  7 Look Carefully
  8 Who's Got It?
  9 Packing a Suitcase
  10 Forbidden Number

Guessing & Puzzling Games
  11 Seeing Black
  12 Riddles, Riddles
  13 Captain's Challenges
  14 Crossword Puzzles
  15 I Spy with my Little Eye
  16 Pictionary
  17 Taboo
  18 If – Then
  19 Who am I?
  20 Guessing Occupations

Games for Playing with Words
  21 Word within a Word
  22 Chain Reaction
  23 Anagrams
  24 To Be Continued
  25 Hand & Foot
  26 Word Chains
  27 Compound Career Choice

Contents

28 Four Letters
29 Hangman
30 Dictionary Game

Thinking Games
31 Always
32 This and That
33 Similarities & Differences
34 Good Relationships
35 Consequences
36 Abbreviations
37 Never Bored Again
38 Oxymorons
39 Everyday Patents
40 That's Logical

Memory Games
41 Memory Chain
42 Film Story
43 Learning Through Movement
44 Body & Soul Learning
45 Mnemonics
46 Remembering Names
47 Visualising
48 Rhyming
49 Number Symbols
50 Pocket Trick

'Surely, one can't engage in anything more clever in this beautiful world than play.'

– Henrik Ibsen

Everyday Observations

There are so many things that we see or use nearly every day, but don't really know them very well.

Who actually knows how many spokes their bicycle wheel has or how many steps there are in their staircase? In order to sharpen the group's perception skills, prepare questions about things relating everyday life and have a group member ask some questions at the beginning of each session.

Remember, the questions should relate to things that are available and familiar to all members of the group.

Example

- How many doors do you walk past in the corridor before you reach this room?
- What does a potato smell like?
- Where on the page in your passport is your photograph?

The number of questions that could be asked is endless. Getting the group to think these up will require as much creativity as answering them.

Feeling is Everything

Perception involves more than just seeing and hearing. Unfortunately, we tend to neglect our other senses and so we need to make an effort to use them.

For this activity the group sits together in a circle with their eyes closed. Then an object is passed from hand to hand and the group must try to guess the identity of the item without talking to each other, using only their sense of touch. Once the item has been returned to the group leader, everybody writes down their guess. Then the next item is passed around. After five rounds, compare answers.

- Who guessed correctly?
- Which items were easy, which were difficult to recognise through touch alone?

Variation

Alternatively, different objects could be passed around the circle inside a bag. Each group member is told to feel for a particular object. If someone thinks that they have found their object they should take it out of the bag and show the group.

This exercise is more difficult than it sounds, especially when the objects are not that different from each other, for example, apples, pears, oranges, kiwis and other fruit of a similar shape, and when the time allowed to find an item is limited.

Perceiving With All the Senses

Give each group member a similar object, for example, apples, pieces of velvet, stones, small boxes full of soil, and so on. The group's task is to try to explore this object using all their senses and then describe it as precisely as possible.

They should look at the object carefully, hold it in their hands and – preferably with their eyes closed – touch and feel the object, smell it, put it to their ears and listen to it, sensing whether the object is rigid or flexible, hard or soft, cold or warm, and so on.

All these perceptions can then be put into words and written down. Afterwards, compare everyone's perceptions.

- Has anybody ever studied an object so intensively by using all their senses?
- Which senses are normally under-used?
- Did everyone experience the same perceptions?
- How do the written descriptions differ from each other?
- Did everyone manage to find suitable words to describe their perceptions?
- Which descriptions are particularly accurate?
- What was difficult to put into words?

Souvenirs

This well-known game is also very good for sharpening the senses. One group member starts by saying: 'My aunt went on holiday to Spain. I wonder what sort of things she has brought back for me.' Now the others have to guess:

- ☼ A T-shirt? No.
- ☼ Sangria? Yes.
- ☼ Mandarins? No.
- ☼ Oranges? No.
- ☼ Seafood? Yes

The challenge is to work out that the aunt is carrying souvenirs that start with 'S' for 'Spain'. If she had been to Austria, she would have brought back things beginning with 'A', from Florida she would brought back things beginning with 'F', and so on.

Variation

The game can be made more difficult if the souvenirs do not have to start with the letter, but instead contain the letter somewhere within the word. In this case, the aunt may also have brought back 'mandarins', 'trousers' or a 'purse' from 'Spain'.

Those group members who have worked out the game's rule should continue playing until everyone has worked it out or decided to give up.

Mum Likes Coffee

This game is actually a variation on the previous one. One group member starts to talk about their 'mum' and her likes and dislikes. The others have to work out the rule that underlies this game by asking questions or by making up their own statements about the 'mum' and asking if they are true or false.

For example, mum not only like coffee, but also apple juice, she likes Danny, but not dad. She likes going swimming, but does not like cycling …, in other words, mum likes anything whose name contains double letters.

Variation

The rule underlying this game doesn't always have to be based on letters or spelling, players could also think of content-based or group-related criteria:

Content-based: Rosie only likes things that can be associated with 'roses', such as thorns, Sleeping Beauty, the colour red and love, but nothing blue, and not lilies, fur cones or Cinderella.

Group-related: An imaginary character who only likes things that begin with the initial letter of the name of the group member whose turn it is.

Obviously

We often find it easier to see what we expect to see rather than what is actually there.

This can be shown by the following activity. One group member leaves the room. Then an everyday item such as an eraser, a glass or something similar is hidden 'in the open' by being placed somewhere where it does not belong and where it is therefore not expected to be.

For example, an eraser could be placed next to the soap on the sink, or a glass could be put on a bookshelf. The choice of hiding place can be varied to alter the difficulty of the game.

Once the object has been 'hidden', call the person outside back into the room. Don't tell them what they should be looking for. While the searcher is looking, the others can give clues by, for example, clapping their hands or humming increasingly loudly when the searcher is getting closer to the object and by becoming quieter the further away they get.

Look Carefully

Tell the group that they are going to have to find things out about their fellow group members using their powers of observation.

Example

- Who is wearing the most jewellery?
- Who is wearing the most black?
- Who has the darkest brown eyes?

Now ask the group to walk around the room and carefully observe everyone else while you play some quiet music.

When the music stops, everyone must place a hand on the shoulder of the person who, in their opinion, meets the criteria of the question. This activity must be based on attributes that are visible to all.

Who's Got It?

One group member must think of a personal characteristic such as 'an earring in the left ear' or 'hair longer than collar length' which has to be worked out by everyone else. Then that person looks at each of the other group members in turn and observes: 'Felix has got it, Maria has, Julia hasn't, Mike hasn't got it, Tim has', and so on.

The first person to work which characteristic is being talked about can select the next one to be guessed. To make the game more difficult, two or more characteristics can be combined, for example, 'blond hair and wearing a watch'.

Packing a Suitcase

This well-known game can be used to reinforce or demonstrate knowledge in nearly every area.

The group sits in a circle. One group member starts: 'I'm packing my suitcase and I'm putting in …'. The next person in the circle repeats this sentence and adds an item of their own, until everyone has put an item into the suitcase.

'Packing a Suitcase' works really well for learning vocabulary. For this purpose, vocabulary relating to a particular subject can be packed into the suitcase.

For example, the group could be working on 'environmentalism' and could use 'Packing a Suitcase' as a topic starter, bringing some humour to a difficult theme:

- 'I am packing my suitcase and I am putting in a full bin bag.'
- 'I am packing my suitcase and I am putting in a full bin bag and a can of smog.'
- 'I am packing my suitcase and I am putting in a full bin bag, a can full of smog and a canister full of aviation fuel.'

Larger groups should split up and pack several suitcases using the same topic, otherwise the game can become too difficult. Once all suitcases have been packed, discuss their different contents in the whole group.

Forbidden Number

The group sits in a circle and decides on a 'forbidden' number, for example, '3'. This number, its multiples – for 3 that would include 6, 9, 12, and so on – and any number combinations containing that number – for 3 that would include 13, 23, 33, etc. – must not be named, but should instead be replaced by 'psst'.

Ask the group to take turns to count around the circle as quickly as possible. Anyone who accidentally says a 'forbidden' number has to sit out a turn or is out of the game altogether.

If the game is used to practice times tables, 'forbidden' numbers should only include multiples and not the number combinations of the number in question.

Variation

The game can be made exciting and challenging even for groups who have mastered their times tables and number combinations by having two 'forbidden' numbers and two substitute sounds, e.g. 'psst' and 'buzz'.

Seeing Black

One group member will appear to have become a mind reader and be able to perceive, with their eyes closed, an object or person being pointed at by someone else!

For example, the second group member is pointing to a remote control. Then they ask the 'mind reader' specific questions:

- Am I pointing at a water glass? No.
- Am I pointing at the clock on the wall? No.
- Am I pointing at the candle? No.
- Am I pointing at the TV remote control? Yes.

The two people must agree on a kind of 'code' beforehand. So, the apparent mind reading ability is down to a simple trick, which the rest of the group have to work out.

The question relating to the item that is being pointed at always follows a question that involves naming a black item – in this case, the TV remote control is black. The pair keep pointing and 'mind reading' until the group works out the code.

Once the group has worked out the 'code', the next pair has to think of a new one. For example, the question leading to the correct answer could be about something round, or refer to a person whose first name contains a certain letter, and so on.

Riddles, Riddles

Funny riddles and conundrums are a useful and very motivating resource for practising logical thinking. You can collect riddles over a period of time by writing them down on index cards. They can then be used for thinking practice as and when there is an opportunity. You will find riddles and conundrums in magazines, newspapers and books.

Even better, ask the group to come up with their own riddles as this requires logical and creative thinking. If they also have to choose a riddle to read aloud, it gives them an opportunity for higher level reading practice and reading comprehension because, if they read carefully, they will usually come up with the answer.

Examples

- What is big on the Queen, but small on the quail? (The 'Q')
- Six family members only have one small umbrella to shelter under, but none of them is getting wet. Why not? (It is not actually raining.)
- Is there a day that does not contain the letter 'a'? (Yes, 'tomorrow')
- What is the largest number of eggs anybody has ever managed to eat on an empty stomach? (One, after that the stomach wouldn't be empty anymore.)
- Which question can never be answered with 'yes'? (Are you asleep?)
- For which activities could we not have someone else stand in for us? (Eating, sleeping)

Captain's Challenges

'Captain's Challenges' are conundrums that contain confusing and irrelevant information in order to make it as difficult as possible to find the correct answer to a simple question.

Example

The Captain is a remarkable man who is 189cm tall and weighs 90 kilos. He got his captain's license when he was 20. Since then he has commanded a large ship. The ship is 60 meters long, has seven rooms and even has three toilets. He uses the ship to go out to sea five times every week. On the second Sunday of every third month he takes out all those passengers who have turned 18 in the last 90 days. He has been commanding the ship for the last 25 years. His youngest son is 22. How old is the captain? (45)

- ☼ How many mistakes did the group make?
- ☼ How long did it take until the last group member had found – and understood – the answer?

Extension

Ask the group to come up with and solve their own 'Captain's Challenges' – the more confusing the better.

Crossword Puzzles

This is an easy way to generate crossword puzzles for any given subject.

To do this, write down a key word or term vertically in capital letters. Staying with the same topic, find words that can be written horizontally and which all contain one letter of the key word. Finally, write definitions or clues for each words. For the final puzzle, draw boxes in place of the letters and only give the group the clues or definitions. For example, if the subject chosen is 'making music', the crossword could look like this:

1	dru **M** s
2	tr **U** mpet
3	bas **S**
4	drum st **I** cks
5	**C** larinet
6	cymb **A** l
7	triang **L** e
8	p **I** ano
9	go **N** g
10	**S** ing
11	conduc **T** or
12	**R** ecorder
13	t **U** ne
14	**M** usic teacher
15	loudsp **E** aker
16	tale **N** t
17	flu **T** e
18	music le **S** son

Clues

1. Percussion instrument made of skin stretched over round hollow frame.
2. Metal wind instrument.
3. Lowest singing part in music.
4. You need these to play a percussion instrument.
5. Woodwind instrument.
6. One of two brass discs struck together to produce a clashing sound.
7. Musical instrument with three angles.
8. Musical instrument with a keyboard.
9. Metal disc which sounds when struck with a soft mallet.
10. To utter sounds or words with musical modulation.
11. Director of the orchestra.
12. Type of flute.
13. Melody.
14. A person educating others about music.
15. Instrument for converting electrical signals into sound audible at a distance.
16. Natural ability.
17. Wind instrument with blowhole on side.
18. Time-tabled session where you learn about music.

Hint

If all the answers are correct, the big boxes in the middle will name a term for the tools which an orchestra could not do without.

Extension

You can split the group into smaller ones, and ask each smaller group to design and then solve a puzzle.

I Spy with my Little Eye

This traditional children's game can be used to test or reinforce all kinds of knowledge without any specific preparation.

One person thinks of a word or an object, it doesn't have to be in the room, and states one of its features. They must be careful not to give too much information away and can be allowed to mislead the others a little, so guessing isn't too easy. The remaining group members have to ask questions to try to work out the word the person is thinking of. The first person to guess the correct answer can be the next to think of a word.

For example, the word to be guessed is 'angel':

- ☼ 'I spy with my little eye something that has wings.'
- ☼ 'Is it a bird?' 'No.'
- ☼ 'Is it an aeroplane?' 'No.'
- ☼ 'Can it actually use its wings to fly?' 'Yes, it can fly…'

Variations

The game can be made easier or more difficult to meet the needs of different groups, e.g. naming objects that can actually be seen. Even pre-school children enjoy playing this game. For younger groups, the game is particularly suitable for building vocabulary or for learning specific concepts such as colours: 'I spy with my little eye something red …'

Equally, the game can still be exciting when played with adults, for example, when more abstract terms such as 'democracy' or 'freedom' have to be described and guessed.

And, of course, the game can also be used to learn vocabulary and practise question and answer forms in any foreign language.

Pictionary®

Write key words relating to a particular subject on separate pieces of paper.

Ask one person to choose a piece of paper and illustrate the word on the paper by drawing it on the board or a flipchart. The rest of the group must try to guess as quickly as possible what is being depicted. The first person to guess then selects a word of their own. If the group is not too large, the game can continue until everyone has had a turn at drawing.

Variation

The game can also be played as a competition. Divide the group into two teams who then play against each other. The group that is quickest at guessing what their team member is drawing gets a point. The group that has the most points after an agreed number of rounds is the winner.

Taboo

Divide the group into smaller ones consisting of about five people. Then provide a topic, for example, 'being gifted'.

Now give each group a piece of paper onto which each person must write a word that relates to the given topic. For example:

- performance
- encouragement
- exceptional
- skilled
- elite

Next, swap the pieces of paper among the groups. Now, each group has to come up with a short written text about the topic, but without using any of the words on the piece of paper they have been given and then read this to the other groups.

Afterwards, one group at a time can be questioned by the others about their text. Allow each group the same amount of question time. Again, answers must not contain any of the taboo words. The questioners must try to use trick questioning in order to break the taboo of the others.

Deduct points for each taboo word spoken. The winner is the group who has the most points.

If – Then

Divide the group into two. Using 'If-Then' sentences, each group must quickly come up with riddles and questions that have to be solved by members of the other group. For example, easy riddles are:

☼ If David is Sonia's uncle, then David's son is her …? (cousin)

☼ If today is Monday, then tomorrow will be …? (Tuesday)

The 'If-Then' riddles can be made more demanding, depending on the ability of the group, for example:

☼ If Sonia is Anna's granddaughter and David's son is Sonia's cousin, then David is Anna's …? (son)

☼ If today was yesterday, then tomorrow would be …? (today)

You can also practise and consolidate themes and topics that are currently being learned by the group through using 'If-Then' riddles.

Who am I?

One group member is sent out of the room. Meanwhile, the others think of a character – from a book, a celebrity, a fairytale character – for that person to guess.

In order to work out their new 'identity', the guesser is only allowed to ask questions that can be answered using 'yes' or 'no'. For example, the guesser cannot ask 'How old am I?', but is allowed to ask, 'Was I born between 1850 and 1900?' Other questions could be: 'Am I a woman?', 'Am I a musician?', 'Am I tall?', 'Is my 100th birthday being celebrated this year?', and so on.

Before starting the activity, decide how many questions may be asked or how much time will be allowed for guessing.

Guessing Occupations

While one group member is outside the room, the others must each choose a different occupation that can be represented by a few simple actions: the carpenter hammering, the dressmaker sewing, the doctor using a stethoscope, the footballer kicking a ball, and so on.

The person who has been called back into the room has to work out which occupation is being represented by which group member. Once someone's occupation has been guessed, they must stop moving.

Extension

If the guesser is unable to guess a particular occupation, the other 'professionals' in the group could down their tools and, instead, mime as many different actions as possible associated with the occupation in question.

Word within a Word

Many words or word combinations hide other words. Finding these hidden words is fun, trains observation and concentration and also means that players have to exercise their brains a little.

Divide into smaller groups. To start with, each small group makes a list of 'words within words' for a given subject on a piece of paper. Subjects could be, for example, first names, animals, numbers, body parts, food and so on. Then the groups exchange pieces of paper and must try to find the words that have been hidden by other groups.

Examples

First names   Graceful
Madam
They performed war dances.
He bent over to tie his shoelace.

Animals   Brat
We must do this again.
He had big antlers.

Numbers   Stone
Weight

Instead of just writing individual words or sentences, the groups could write short stories containing 'hidden words' for others to find.

Chain Reaction

The group sits in a circle, each with a pen and paper.

Each person writes down a topic-based word or answer to a question at the top of their sheet and passes it to the player sitting to their left. That person reads what has been written, folds the paper so it can not be read and writes another associated word. Then the paper is passed on again and is added to by the next player and so on until it has returned to the first player.

Example

The topic might be 'holidays'. The first person writes 'going abroad'. The second person reads it, folds the paper and writes 'flying'. The third person reads the word, folds the paper and writes 'airport', and so on.

Once the round has been completed, the pieces of paper are unfolded and read out. The lists can then be pinned up on a board and, similar to the result of a brainstorm, be used for further work.

Variations

Rather than tell everyone the theme, ask the first person to think of a word and then following group members must write a word they associate with the one they have read. The resulting list can be discussed by the group afterwards.

Anagrams

Explain to the group what an anagram is – a word or words whose letters can be rearranged to make a new word or words with a different meaning.

For example, the letters of the group members' names can be rearranged to create a pseudonym, which could then be used within the group instead of real names.

Examples

- Steven Spielberg – Best pin legs ever
- Elvis Presley – Silver spy eel
- Harry Potter – Trophy rater

Of course, all sorts of different anagrams can be made. Using the names of living creatures and everyday objects, the group could create 'new' names; for example, 'chinchilla' can be become 'challichin' or 'newspaper' could become 'warn peeps'.

Note

Finding anagrams is actually not very easy. It can take some time to play around with the letters of a word in order to come up with something new that makes at least a little sense. This activity represents a real thinking challenge and is good fun at the same time.

To Be Continued

This game encourages creative imagination and fluency. It can be carried out sitting at desks or in a circle.

One group member thinks of a subject – the sillier or more absurd the better. The next person begins to tell the story. After a few sentences the next person takes over and continues to tell the story. The story telling continues around the circle – the last person in the circle must conclude the story.

Variation

If the group is a lively one with group members who are able to contribute spontaneously, such stories can be told without any predetermined order. If someone can think of an original continuation they can raise their hand and then continue the story. The story can continue for as long as the group members feel like story telling.

Hand & Foot

We can do a lot more with our bodies than we think we might be able to or are aware that we can. For example, what can we do by just using our hands or feet?

The group members sit or stand in a circle. They take it in turns to make a movement with their hand or foot, but it has to be one that has not been made by anybody else in the circle. The others have to try and name the action that has been portrayed as accurately as they can.

Example

- A hand can:
  hit, point, stroke, push, pinch

- A foot can:
  kick, stand, wave, stamp, caress

The game can also use other body parts. However, the movements of some body parts, such as the head, are obviously limited.

Instead of stopping after going around once, the group could keep going and try to find as many different actions as possible for a hand, a foot, or any other body part.

Extension

An extension of this game involves collecting saying and idioms that contain the words 'hand' and 'foot', such as:

- hand over fist
- lend a hand
- foot the bill
- put your foot in it

It can also be interesting to collect such saying in different languages.

- Are some sayings the same in every language?
- If not, how are they different and why?

Word Chains

This well-known activity can be used to extend group members' vocabulary through the creative use of words. Ensure the group know what a compound word is – a word made up of two shorter ones.

Group members sit in a circle. One person thinks of a compound word. The next player now has to think of another compound word that starts with the second part of the first word.

Example

forearm – armchair – chairman – manhole – …

Continue the word chain for as long as possible. The group could count how many links they manage in a given chain, and then use this as a target to beat by at least one more word in the next round.

Variations

The game doesn't have to be played with compound words. It could also be played so that the last letter in a word has to become the initial letter of the next word. The players could agree to use only words that relate to a particular subject, for example, food – fruits, vegetables, sports – football, tennis.

Compound Career Choice

Many more jobs and careers exist than the group could possibly think of – and these are some that haven't yet been invented. From definitions, the group members have to guess occupations, some well-known and some obscure, all of which are compound words.

Example

- A gardening business is looking for someone who is good at cutting grass. Which occupation could that be? (lawnmower)
- A circus has a vacancy for someone who is good at flinging fire. What is his title? (flamethrower)
- A restaurant is missing someone who is able to do all the washing up. Who are they looking for? (dishwasher)

No doubt the group will think of many more occupations and job descriptions, some of which might be quite unusual.

Four Letters

One group member thinks of a word consisting of four letters and writes it down on a piece of paper. The others now have to try to guess the word as quickly as possible while following certain rules.

In order to work out the four correct letters quickly, group members need a reasonable vocabulary and ability to think of words, as well as the ability to skilfully combine letters.

All group members need pencil and paper. To start with, each group member must write down the letters of the alphabet as well as the following:

Solution   Letters included

_ _ _ _   _____

For example, the four-letter word to be guessed is 'list'. One group member now suggests a four-letter solution: 'Is the word "sand"?' Answer: 'No, but it does contain the letter "s".' Now the group members cross out 's' in their alphabet and are not allowed to ask for 's' again. Then they add the letter to their table:

Solution   Letters included

_ _ _ _   s_____

The next question could be: 'Is the word "mast"?' Answer: 'No, but the word does contain the letter "t" in the same place as 'mast'.' Now group members cross out 't' in their alphabet and add it to their table:

Solution	Letters included
_ _ _ t	s

Players continue to suggest four-letter words until they have found the right one.

Variation

If anyone suggests a word containing a letter that has already been crossed out, without guessing the correct word, they are out.

Hangman

One person thinks of an unusual word containing as many letters as possible. A dash is drawn on a large piece of paper or the board for each letter. The initial letter is written in, and anywhere else it occurs within the word.

Now the others have to guess the word by suggesting letters. Every time an incorrect letter is guessed, the 'hangman' grows a little more, starting with the gallows. The group has to try to guess the word before the hangman is complete. For more able groups all spaces can be left blank at the beginning of the game.

For example, the word to be guessed is 'aeroplanes'.
'A _ _ _ _ _ a _ _ _' is written on the piece of paper. The first letter guessed is 'u' and the base of the gallows is drawn. Then 't' and most of the gallows is drawn. The next letter to be guessed is 'e' and is written in place on the piece of paper, and so on.

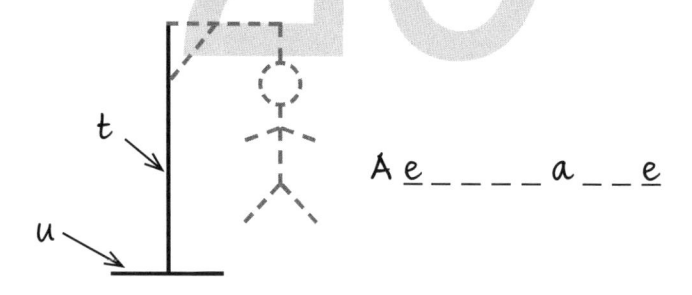

A e _ _ _ _ a _ _ e

This way, even practising spellings can be fun. Instead of guessing single words, players could also guess terminology, phrases or expressions and so on that are linked to a given topic.

Dictionary Game

As the game's title suggests, the group members will need age-appropriate dictionaries for this game as well as pens and paper.

Split the group into two teams, who will become the 'questions' and 'answers' teams for the first round. The 'questions' team must choose ten obscure words from the dictionary and prepare multiple-choice definitions for these. The wrong definitions should be as vexing and distracting as possible.

Examples

☼ A *Patriot* is
    a) a person that loves their country
    b) a founding father
    c) a citizen of Patros

☼ *Rachitis* is
    a) a form of tonsillitis
    b) a girl's name
    c) a deficiency disease involving a lack of Vitamin B

Points can be given for each correct answer. Once the list of ten words is completed, the teams can swap. The winner is the group that has the most points after an agreed number of rounds.

Variation

The game can be made easier if played as follows:

The group sits in a circle. The dictionary is passed around the circle and players take it in turn to point to a word with their eyes closed, which then has to be defined by the player to their left.

Always

For this activity the players require pens and paper. One group member has to ask questions beginning 'What is always …', for which the others have to think of as many answers as possible within a set time.

Example

- What is always red? (a stop light, blood, red wine)
- What is always bigger than a human being? (house, aircraft hangar, aeroplane)

At the end, read out and compare the answers.

- Are they all really 'correct'?
- Can the group always spot a correct answer or do some need a bit more thought?

This and That

Within a set time the group members have to think up as many objects or animals that meet two criteria at the same time.

Example

☼ Red and inedible (toadstool, red hair, ladybird)

☼ Round and warm (baked apples, bowl of soup, fluffy chick)

At the end the number and originality of the group's answers can be discussed.

Similarities & Differences

Choose one group member to name two objects or animals. The rest of the group have to work out what the two things have in common and how they are different.

Depending on how the 'pairs' are selected, the task can be made easier or more difficult and the answers will be more or less original as a result.

Example

☼ What are the similarities and differences between a newspaper and a lamp?

   ☼ *Similarities:* Both can be lit, both can be enlightening, and so on.

   ☼ *Differences:* The lamp can be plugged in; the newspaper can be used to wrap something up, and so on.

Discuss the number and originality of the group's answers after the activity.

Good Relationships

Quickly read to the group a list of between 20 and 30 nouns. For each word, the group members must write down a second word that is linked in some way to the first.

Example

- ☼ ship — captain
- ☼ car — wheel
- ☼ glass — water
- ☼ clock — time

Afterwards compare the words the group has come up with. Were any particularly original?

Sources for word lists

Word lists for this sort of exercise can be compiled easily by choosing any text, for example, a newspaper article or a page from a book, and simply reading out the nouns. Other word types can be chosen instead of nouns.

Variation

As quickly as possible, group members must find a third word that is somehow linked to two randomly chosen nouns. Again, words from any text can be used as starting words.

Example

- ☼ ship, car — transport
- ☼ car, glass — windscreen
- ☼ water, time — ferry timetable

Each person can read out their answers at the end — any associations that do not make sense to everyone should be explained.

Consequences

Ask the group to think up as many consequences for a particular wish or hope within a set amount of time. 'I wish it would be more sunny.' 'I want to win the lottery.'

Example

What are the consequences of a lottery win?

- Becoming rich.
- Travelling around the world.
- Starting to drink once the money runs out.

What consequences would continuous sunshine have?

- Everyone would have the same colour skin: brown.
- Water might run out.
- People would have to take more holidays because it will be too hot to work.

Award points for the number and originality of suggestions. Alternatively, the suggestions could become the basis for extended discussions.

- Who could have guessed the number and type of consequences of a 'simple wish' like wanting more sunshine?
- Would we actually be any happier if certain wishes were to come true?
- Is there anything that can be done to limit negative consequences?

Abbreviations

Abbreviations feature increasingly often in our lives. Frequently we don't bother to use a complete word or sentence, but instead limit ourselves to an abbreviation. Some abbreviations have become so familiar that we don't know what they stand for anymore. Discuss abbreviations that are commonly used.

Abbreviations can be used for creative thinking activities. To start with, give the group the meaning of an abbreviation, then ask them to come up with a new meaning.

Example

☼ IQ?

☼ Actual meaning: 'Intelligence Quotient'.

☼ New meaning: 'Inland Quark' or 'Island Quest'

☼ YMCA?

☼ Actual meaning: 'Young Men's Christian Association'

☼ New meaning: 'You Mean Crab Apples' or 'Yes, My Cuddly Ape'

Variation 1

This game can also be played as a quiz. Divide into small groups. One group prepares some questions by choosing an abbreviation and coming up with three possible definitions, one real and two made-up. The other group have to try and guess the real meaning.

/... continued

Example

What does C&DH mean?

- ☼ Cat and dog handling
- ☼ Command and data handling
- ☼ Career and development hierarchy

Variation 2

Another variation of this game is to use random letter sequences to form abbreviations (perhaps sourced from the letters on car number plates), and then ask the group to formulate sentences.

Example

CA – ATB: Carrots And Turnips Are The Best.
WU – TYC: What's Up? Tickle Your Child.

Never Bored Again

Within a set time, ask group members to write down everything they might do to occupy themselves during a long train journey. These can be serious or fun, real or imaginary.

Example

- Read
- Sleep
- Pick your nose
- Do relaxation exercises
- Fall in love

- Who had the most ideas?
- Which ideas were particularly original?
- Has anyone actually tried any of these things?
- Which can be recommended?

This anti-boredom game can also be played competitively by giving points for the number or originality of ideas. It can also be used to make other 'boring' times more exciting.

Example

- What could you do during boring lessons?
- What could you do in a long queue at a checkout?
- What could you do if it rains for three days during the holidays?

Oxymorons

An oxymoron is a figure of speech that combines two normally contradictory terms. Challenge the group members to work together, or on their own, to come up with as many oxymorons as possible within a given time.

Example

- The living dead
- A black bull seeing red
- A precise estimate
- A deafening silence

Oxymorons are very often used in an ironic context.

Example

- Good airline food
- A train timetable
- Military intelligence

It is not actually very easy to come up with oxymorons when you try to think of them. How many oxymorons can group members come up with in, for example, 15 minutes?

Everyday Patents

Products can always be improved. Challenge the group to think of clever ways to improve everyday objects.

Examples

- A fountain pen that combines ink and an eraser in one. By pressing a button on the fountain pen, the flow of ink can be stopped and the eraser can be activated. No more annoying crossing out and having to start again.

- A car tyre that senses when the road gets slippery, or when it get a puncture or when it is low on air. This would avoid many accidents.

The group members could also illustrate their ideas by drawing or making a model which needs to show the improvement but does not actually have to work!

The group can do some further research on their ideas.

- Have some of their suggestions for products already been thought up?

- Which might actually be possible?

- Who could the group talk to about their 'patent' suggestions?

- Who might be interested?

- What skills have group members discovered in themselves during this activity?

That's Logical

Most people will agree with the saying 'There is an exception to every rule'.

However, if this saying is true, then it would follow that there are rules that do not allow exceptions, because, if a rule says that there are always exceptions, then the rule that all rules have exception must itself have an exception!

Ask the group to invent and solve logical problems.

Example

In a group of children, all the boys have blue eyes and some children with blue eyes also have brown hair.

Which of the following statements are then true?

a) All boys have brown hair.

b) Some of the children with brown hair are boys.

c) All children with brown hair who do not have blue eyes are not boys.

d) All children with blue eyes are boys.

e) Some children with blue eyes are boys.

(Answer: b, c, e)

Memory Chain

Memorising meaningful and contextually-linked information is always easier than trying to remember a list of random words. So, if a meaningful link does not exist, we can invent our own.

This is how it works. Using the imagination, the words to be learned can be combined into a story, making sure the original order of words is maintained in the story.

Example

- ☼ The task is to remember the venues for the first three Olympic Games of modern times: Athens – Paris – St Louis.
- ☼ Our story could be as follows: Athene went to Paris, where she was going to meet the Holy Louis.

Divide into small groups to come up with memory chains related to certain subjects or events.

Film Story

A list of words to be remembered can be used to make up a story that is as funny and original as possible. In this way, a special memory effect is created, because instead of trying to remember and recall individual items, we can make an imaginary film, which can later be replayed scene by scene in our minds, making the camera move slowly from one scene to the next.

Example

The group needs to memorise the disciplines of modern pentathlon 'riding, fencing, shooting, swimming and running'. Using these words we can shoot the following scenes for a Western.

- ☼ Our hero Joe is fencing with five villains.
- ☼ He runs to his horse.
- ☼ The villains shoot at him.
- ☼ Joe rides for his life.
- ☼ He swims across the river and collapses safely on the opposite river bank.

Learning Through Movement

Traditionally, it has been thought that a correct learning position involves sitting 'properly' on a chair with a book on the table in front of you. However, it seems that movement can actually facilitate learning and remembering.

For example, when learning vocabulary or sentence structure in a foreign language, it is helpful to not only read through the words or phrases and to say them out aloud and write them down, but also to make movements or actions that correspond with or are linked to different words or phrases.

Example

If the sentence 'I walk to the window' is to be learned in German, in addition to memorising 'Ich gehe zum Fenster', students can also carry out the corresponding action. If someone actually walks to the window at the same time as saying the sentence, they can be more likely to remember it.

If it isn't possible to actually carry out the corresponding action, it should at least be mimed. The term 'autofahren', i.e., 'to drive a car' in German, can be anchored in the memory by simultaneously turning an imaginary steering wheel while saying the word.

If the group learns together using movements and actions, everyone will stimulate their brains as well as having lots of fun!

Body & Soul Learning

We remember best when we try to perceive something using as many senses as possible. We can see and hear something, feel and smell it and, in our imaginations, let it dissolve on our tongues and also imagine it in action. By doing so, we can think about and understand what we have to learn and be moved by it.

This method is particularly suitable for memorising poetry. For example, is the action taking place in a forest? In our imagination we can conjure up the smell of the forest and feel the bark of the trees. Is there a hiker in the poem? We can take a few steps and accompany him on his way for a little while. Is the hiker waving his hat? We can pretend to be waving our hats, and so on.

Nearly every poem provides an opportunity for holistic learning. The group can practise this together in smaller groups. Afterwards the poems can be acted out and presented to the whole group.

Mnemonics

A good method for learning new information is to make up simple, memorable sentences using the initial letters of the information to be learned. If possible, there should be a link between the sentence and the information to be memorised. However, this isn't always necessary, sometimes strange associations work best. Mnemonics can be used for remembering key information in different subjects.

Example

This mnemonic helps to memorise the nine planets of our solar system – Mercury, Venus, Earth, Mars, Jupiter, Saturn, Uranus, Neptune, Pluto – in the correct sequence starting with the planet closest to the sun.

☼ *My very easy method just speeds up naming planets.*

To remember the names of the seven continents of the earth – Europe, Antarctica, Asia, Africa, Australia, North America, South America – try the following:

☼ *Eat An Aspirin After A Naff Sandwich*

This mnemonic helps to remember how to spell the start of 'beautiful':

☼ *Big elephants are ugly individuals.*

Thinking up mnemonics to help memorise information is not always easy. It generally requires quite a lot of creative thinking, with the result that even the process of coming up with a mnemonic within a group can help people remember the information to be learned.

Remembering Names

Many people have problems remembering other people's names. The most important requirement for remembering a name is having a genuine interest in the person whose name we are trying to remember. In addition, memory for names can be facilitated using specific memory strategies.

Names can be linked with pictures and other associations. This is easy if someone is called 'Carpenter' or 'Foote', but other names, too, can be visualised. For example:

☼ Mr Stoneman can appear in our mind's eye as a man throwing stones.

☼ Mrs Forkner is a lady who always eats using a fork.

Alternatively, we could think of specific physical characteristics:

☼ Mrs Red can be thought of with red hair.

☼ Mr Otto could be thought of with O-shaped legs.

Other associations can be created by playing with a name; for example:

☼ Mr Olney has old knees.

☼ Mr Rolls drives a Rolls Royce.

A Warning

If such mnemonics for names are being thought up within a group, and especially for group members' names, special attention must be paid to ensure that associations are funny and original, but never hurtful or offensive.

Visualising

Memorising more difficult and/or more abstract words or terminology becomes easier when these are 'translated' into concrete visual images.

Let's say we cannot remember the term 'Polaroid Camera', so we can try to think of a visualisation. Imagining 'Paula rolls the camera' is likely to stick in our memory much better.

Or the symbols '<' for 'smaller than' and '>' for 'larger than' keep getting mixed up.

'<' : The mouth of the crocodile wraps itself around the baby deer, which becomes smaller as it is eaten.

'>': When the mouth of the crocodile snaps closed without catching its prey the deer has the chance to grow larger.

Acting this out using the arms will further increase the likelihood that the group will remember what the two symbols mean. Group members can think up their own visualisations and tell the group. This way, people will receive plenty of stimulation for their own memory work.

Rhyming

Information that rhymes is easier to memorise than information that does not rhyme. Here is an example of how to use rhyme to memorise information:

'In fourteen hundred and ninety-two,
Columbus sailed the ocean blue.'

The following rhymes have proved themselves when learning spellings:

'I before E except after C'
'When two vowels go walking, the first one does the talking.'

Ask the group to try to come up with rhymes for other important facts. A good way of practising the use of rhymes for memorising information involves learning the birthdays of group members:

- ☼ Julia's birthday is on the 8th of March – Eight and three? Julia ate a bee.

- ☼ Freddy's birthday is on the 31st of July – July is over, Freddy travels to Dover.

We can also use this method to better remember names of people, other animals and objects, for example:

- ☼ Mr Towers loves flowers.

- ☼ Mammals include camels.

- ☼ The hoe hurt my toe.

Thinking of poems within a group doesn't just facilitate learning and strengthen the ability to remember things, it is also great fun, especially if rhymes are allowed to become ridiculous.

Number Symbols

If someone has difficulty memorising numbers, they should try this trick.

Each number from 1 to 10 is given a symbol that has as much physical similarity with its number as possible.

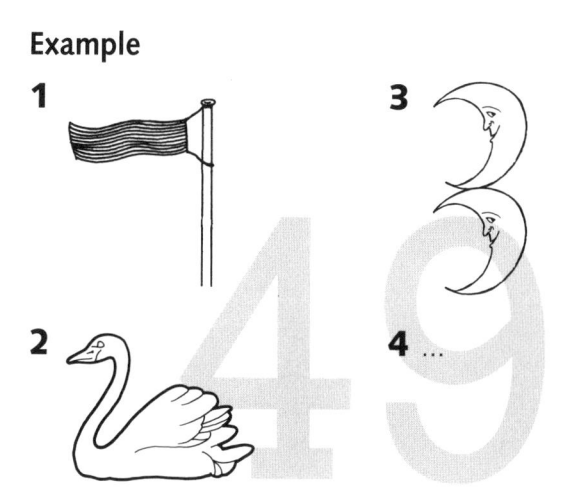

Example

1

2

3

4 ...

Ask each group member to think of their own symbols. Alternatively, the group can think up a list of symbols together, maybe finding more than one for each number. Now each person can pick the symbols that match their own personal associations and that they can therefore remember well.

Now, every time someone wants to memorise a number or date they can recall the corresponding pictures. Attaching one or more pictures to a specific number makes it easier to remember and recall that number.

Memory Games

Pocket Trick

If someone has to give a speech or presentation and is not allowed to use notes, e.g., during an oral exam, or doesn't want use written prompts, they can try out the following 'pocket trick' for dealing with mental blocks and memory gaps.

While preparing for the talk or oral exam, collect together a few small objects that feel different when touched, for example, a coin, a paperclip, a marble, a match and so on.

To start with, take the coin, turn and feel it between the fingers and, at the same time, link it to a specific key word or concept. Then take the paperclip, finger it and link it to another key word, and so on.

Once every key word has been linked to a specific object, place the objects in the pocket of the clothes to be worn during the talk or oral exam. If you get stuck, reach into the pocket and feel the different objects. This will help recall of the points linked to the different objects.

This 'pocket trick' can be practised within the group by, for example, using objects to give little talks in front of the group. Such practice runs will help people to feel comfortable and confident in using this method when it really counts.